Friendship is one of our most valuable gifts. It completes our desire to realize our capacity to love. It brings to our lives that closeness that makes us feel connected and whole and that lets us know we are not alone in the world.

Titles by Marci
Published by
Blue Mountain Arts®

Friends Are Forever
A Gift of Inspirational Thoughts to Thank You for Being My Friend

To My Daughter
Love and Encouragement to Carry with You on Your Journey Through Life

To My Granddaughter
A Gift of Love and Wisdom to Always Carry in Your Heart

To My Sister
A Gift of Love and Inspiration to Thank You for Being My Sister

To My Son
Love and Encouragement to Carry with You on Your Journey Through Life

Friends Are Forever

A Gift of Inspirational Thoughts to Thank You for Being My Friend

Marci

Blue Mountain Press™
Boulder, Colorado

Dedicated to my sister Jeri
who is always there with whatever
I need and is my best friend.
I love you!

Library of Congress Control Number: 2010917474
ISBN: 978-1-68088-505-7 (previous ISBN: 978-1-59842-601-4)

Printed in China.
Second printing of this edition: 2024

This book is printed on recycled paper.

This book is printed on paper that has been specially produced to be acid free (neutral pH) and contains no groundwood or unbleached pulp. It conforms with the requirements of the American National Standards Institute, Inc., so as to ensure that this book will last and be enjoyed by future generations.

Blue Mountain Arts, Inc.
P.O. Box 4549, Boulder, Colorado 80306

Contents

Friends Are Forever

We Have Shared So Much Through the Years

Each time I see you, I am reminded of how special our friendship is. It doesn't seem to matter how long it has been between visits, as we pick up right where we left off. We have shared so much through the years... our hopes, our dreams, our joys, and our struggles. Thank you for being a part of my life.

I'll Always Be Grateful

for Our Friendship

As I travel my journey through life, I try to remember to be grateful for the things that are really important. I want you to know that one of the greatest blessings in my life is my friendship with you. You are the person I call when I need to talk, and I know that you will be there sometimes to "just listen." You are the person that I can laugh with about the most important life events. You "know me," and that saves words sometimes... I'm so grateful to share a friendship with you.

You Will Always Have a Place

in My Heart

Our hearts have grown closer with the passing of time. Through the ups and downs of life, we've come to understand what it means to have each other. Sometimes we talk often... sometimes not. It doesn't seem to matter — the feelings of closeness remain with me because I know you are always there. What a blessing it is to have you in my life.

Some people have a way of brightening someone's day... and it's with little things that mean so much. There is a phone call at just the right time, a hug when it is needed, or a comforting word of encouragement.

That special person is you! Your kind and generous spirit shines brightly in my life. Thanks you for all you do and all you are.

I Could Never Find a Better Friend

...Than You

If I searched the world, I could never find a better friend. You are a perfect example of loving and caring and compassion and concern. Just talking to you makes me feel better, and being with you reminds me of the most important things in life. Knowing that I have a friend like you is truly wonderful!

You're Always There When I Need You

Some days I just need a hand to hold… Some days I just need a hug… Some days I just need a word of encouragement… Some days I just need someone to be there for a laugh and a memory… On my "some days" there is you!

Wherever I go... Whatever I do... I carry your friendship in my heart. You give me hope and make life's challenges bearable. You inspire me to do my best. Your friendship stays in my heart each and every hour of the day and reminds me that I am not alone.

An Angel Has Blessed My Life

...With Your Friendship

The blessings of an angel come in many ways. Sometimes these gifts are right before us, and it is only through time that we realize just how blessed we are. You are always there to share a laugh, and you are always ready to tell me everything will be okay when I'm down. I have come to appreciate these simple blessings. You are an angel in my life.

You Are My Friend...

My Soul Mate

You and I, my friend, are two hearts traveling in the same direction. We have one of those rare connections that gives us such a beautiful relationship. So often you know my thoughts before I say them or sense what I need before I ask. Surely God's infinite plan has put you in my path... and selected you to be my friend!

You Are Everything a Friend Should Be ...and More

A friend's love is a gift that you unwrap a little bit each year.

A friend is a mirror of things to come and a reflection of things gone by.

A friend shows you the road before you and knows the path you've taken.

A friend is the one you call when you need to talk to someone who knows your heart.

A friend walks beside you to share each day... stands beside you when you question yourself... and walks in front of you when you've lost your way.

A friend sees your beautiful spirit shining through on good days and bad.

I'm so glad you are my friend!

There Is a Reason

Our Lives Were Brought Together

You are always ready to share with me your experience, strength, and hope, and when I need your guidance, you offer me your wisdom and your understanding. You are there through the good times and a constant light through the bad. When I think about the things that are important to me, I always think of you.

I Treasure Your Presence

in My Life

I have watched you cultivate your unique talents and have been inspired to do the same. I have watched you live with integrity, and this example has led the way. I have accepted the challenge to be my best self, as your encouraging words lifted me up. Watching you handle the ups and downs of life, and seeing you move always to higher ground, gives me a vision of my future.

Friendship Means...

Friendship means never having to face the challenges of life alone.

Friendship means sharing a closeness of spirit that gives life meaning.

Friendship means having a witness to life's tiny, special moments that are so much better when shared.

Friendship means that there is someone who understands where you've been, knows where you want to go, and accepts you for who you are.

Thank you for all that you give so freely and for showing me the true meaning of friendship!

Our Friendship

Was Meant to Be

A lifetime yields only a few lasting friendships. It happens when two special people meet and connect heart and soul. There develops an understanding of what is in each other's heart that transcends words... there is a nurturing of the spirit that is mutual... there is an exchange of love and support that is essential... and there is a sense of belonging and knowing that their friendship was meant to be.

It's Rare to Find a Friend

as Special as You

So many times I think of you, and I experience all over again the special times we have had. I remember a laugh we shared, and I smile; I remember the love and support you offered, and I feel thankful. I think about how important friendships are in a world where everything else seems so uncertain, and I know I am truly blessed! Good friends like you are a rare treasure. It is a gift to have you as mine!

You Make Everything in My Life

So Much Better

You are there with love,
encouragement, or a hug,
and somehow you always seem
to know just what I need.
When I am down, you lift me
up, forgiving my mistakes and
helping me forget them, too...
When I need encouragement,
you let me know that I
am not alone...

When I need a hug, you wrap your arms around me and tell me everything will be okay... When there are good times, we laugh and they are so much better... and when we share sorrow, it seems half as bad.

When I look back, I realize that you had such an impact on my life — one you may not have realized. I want you to know that your kind spirit and loving heart have touched me in a special way with a lasting impression called friendship!

You're More Than a Friend...

You're like Family

You have taught me that what makes a "family" is not found in a name, it is found in the heart. You are so much more to me than a friend... you are like family. You are always there, believing in my dreams and reminding me to believe in them. You are a part of every joy that comes my way, and I am so happy to have you in my life.

You Are That One Special Friend to Me

I Don't Know What I'd Do Without You

We all need that one special person to connect with in a way that transcends ordinary friendship. We need that special someone with whom we can share life's innermost secrets. We need that friend to laugh with over absolutely nothing, and we need to know a hug is ready and waiting on the worst of days. I can find all of these things in you... You are that one special friend to me.

I'm So Glad We Have Each Other

When I think of you, I think, "What could be better than having someone to talk to who already knows all about me and loves me as I am?"

When I think of you, I think, "What could be more fun than sharing my joys with someone who is truly happy for me?"

When I think of you, I think,
"What could be better than a
friendship that has created so
many wonderful memories?"

When I think of you, I think,
"We're friends!" and I realize
how lucky I am to have you!

We Share a Special Connection

Our Bond Is Everlasting

Some days you come into my mind just as the phone rings... and it is you! It is as though you heard or felt my thoughts and knew I needed to talk. Your timely phone call reminds me you are always there, and your understanding reminds me of what a good friend you are. Thank you for loving me... thank you for making me laugh... and thank you for the special connection we share. The bond we have found is everlasting!

My Hopes for You...

May the good things you have brought to my life be returned to you.

May your guardian angel always watch over you and whisper life's secrets in your ear.

May your steps be guided through all of life's challenges and your heart remember its true calling.

May you be blessed with all the things that will bring you lasting happiness.

May faith guide your path toward your dreams... may hope be a constant light in your life... and may love warm your heart every day.

The Road of Life Has Many Turns

Just Take It One Day at a Time

Sometimes the road of life takes us to a place we had planned... Sometimes it shows us a surprise around the bend we could never have anticipated. We make decisions based on the information we have... We accept the ups and downs as they come... We live "one day at a time"... But often we find it is only when we look back that we can see that what we had thought was a "wrong turn" has brought us to exactly the right place and every step was a right one after all!

Remember These Things...

Remember, you are special... there are talents locked away inside you just waiting for the right time to unfold.

Remember to dream... dreams are the start of every great adventure. When you close your eyes and imagine your "happy and successful self in the future," you are beginning your journey!

Remember to listen to your heart... your heart is where your courage lies. When you follow your heart you may meet challenges, but each of your steps will be guided.

Remember, "today" is always the most important day... enjoy every moment of it.

You Are an Inspiration to So Many

...but Especially to Me

Everyone needs someone to look up to... a model of how to find one's calling and follow that dream! You are such an inspiration to so many... You have demonstrated how to move forward in spite of obstacles... how to stay the course when things get tough... and how to keep close to your heart the things that are really important in life on the journey toward success. You have shown that with determination, commitment, and a willingness to share, all your dreams will come true!

Always Follow Your Dream

Your life holds for you endless possibilities. You have built a solid foundation, and you have worked hard for it. Continue to do what is necessary to move forward one day at a time. Write down your dream and tuck it away — entrusting that all things will come at the right time.

Keep sight always of what is important in life. Remember that true happiness and purpose will be found in relationships — in the workplace and at home. Live each day open to guidance, and your purpose will be revealed to you. May your future be filled with love and acceptance.

I Am Proud to Call You

My Friend

You handle life's ups and downs with grace and even remember to encourage others along the way. You face challenges with courage, compassion, and conviction. I am proud to call you my friend.

Kindred Spirits

That's What
We Are!

Some things change with time... some things never do. The way I feel when I spend time with you is one of those constant good things in my life. There is a sense of feeling understood... there is a sense of feeling loved and supported... and there is a deep sense of gratitude as I realize I have been given the wonderful gift of a kindred spirit. Thank you for staying close to my heart... thank you for a friendship that endures... and thank you for sharing your beautiful spirit with me.

You always understand what is in my heart. You are there whenever I need you, listening and offering your insights. You look deeply enough to really see me, allowing me to understand the true meaning of friendship.

It's friends like you who remind me that life's most precious gifts are free. The memories that we create fulfill the promise of love. Thank you for each and every day that you have been my friend and for the memories that live in my heart forever.

You Are Always in My Prayers

May God's Love Be With You Always

You are always in my prayers, and I wanted you to know so that you will be open to the grace that comes your way. I have asked that you feel the love of God like a gentle breeze when you need inspiration... that your faith remain unwavering through all of life's challenges... and that hope be the burning light that always guides your way.

If you ever get discouraged, remember I am thinking of you... believing in you... praying for you... and hoping you know that no matter how big a problem seems or how hopeless you feel, you are never alone, as God's grace is only one request away!

We may not always know the right thing to do or the right path to take, but "faith" will show us the way. Remember that we are never alone, as God is always there to answer prayers and send us the help we need. Sometimes it is "we" who do not recognize that help. Believe, trust, and pray… and know that all your needs will be taken care of.

Dear Friend

You Are Stronger Than You Realize

There are times in our lives when we face a hardship that we do not think we can bear. We wonder, "Why," and we look for a reason to help make sense of it all. Sometimes all we can do is try to come to a place of acceptance and reach out to others who understand what we've been through. Often it is then, as we share our wisdom, strength, and hope, that we get a small glimpse of a larger plan... one that enables us to feel connected... one that shows us that love blesses the giver and the receiver... and one that allows us to see how really strong we are.

Five Keys to Happiness

1. Realize that happiness is a choice... you can make the decision to "be happy" each day.

2. Remember that happiness is contagious. Make someone smile, and the good feelings come right back to you.

3. Be grateful for the little things in life that are free. Make a list, and add to it each morning.

4. Believe that ultimately everything happens for a reason. Acceptance leads the way to happiness.

5. Give away some courage every day! When you encourage another to "keep going," "hang in there," or "believe in their dreams," you will find an unending source of happiness.

I've Learned So Many Important Lessons

That I Want to Share with You

Big problems can be solved in small steps.

When you are still, the gentle voice from within will guide you... listen carefully.

Remember to pray, and let God take the burden of worry from your heart.

Accept that we each learn life's lessons in our own way.

Your Friendship Is like an Angel's Wings...

Lifting Me Up at Just the Right Time

You are always there... to help me fix the bad things, appreciate the little things, and remind me that the most important things in life are free! Your encouraging words and your faith in me are gifts beyond measure.

No Matter How Busy Life Gets...

You Are Always in My Heart

In today's world, life gets so busy that the days roll by and we realize we have not spoken to the ones we love! I want you to know that you are always in my heart... You are one of the most important people in my life, and even if we do not speak every day, my best thoughts and love are always with you.

It is easy to lose track of time. The days pass, and then one day we realize we have lost touch with someone special. So often you are in my thoughts, and I smile thinking of the many memories we have shared. I treasure our talks and our special connection.

Just know that neither time nor distance changes the closeness I feel in my heart when I think of you. You are such an important part of my life... always ready to be part of whatever is happening... always open to listening... always there to share a laugh or dry some tears. And I am always so grateful to have you as my friend!

No Matter What...

I Want Us to Always Stay Close

Friendship is one of life's greatest treasures, and it is a gift that lasts a lifetime. We created a bond during a time in our lives when our beliefs and our experiences were shaping who we were. That bond cannot be broken by the passing of time, even when life gets so busy that we lose touch. I want you to know I think of you often... and you will always have a special place in my heart.

Longtime Friends

Time Spent with Friends
Creates Lifelong
Sweet Memories

Every time we're together, precious moments come flooding back, and I am reminded of all our laughter and joy through the years. I am so appreciative of those times and for having met you. Through the pain and sorrow, happiness and joy, we have learned much. Yours is the humor I can always count on and the friendship I know will last forever.

My Wishes for You

I wish you a life filled with love... a true love to share your every dream... family love to warm your heart... and priceless love found in the gift of friendship.

I wish you peace... peace in knowing who you are... peace in knowing what you believe in... and peace in the understanding of what is important in life.

I wish you joy... joy as you awaken each day with gratitude in your heart for new beginnings... joy when you surrender to the beauty of a flower or a baby's smile... and joy, a hundred times returned, for each time you've brought happiness to another's heart.

Thanks

for All the Little Things You Do

Sometimes I forget to say "thanks" for all the little things you do... but I want you to know that even when I do not say so, I am so thankful for your thoughtfulness, your caring, your willingness to please. Your efforts never go unnoticed, and I thank you!

Your Friendship Has Made

Such a Difference in My Life

There are people who change our lives, often without even realizing the impact they have made just by being themselves. You have made such a difference in my life. I am grateful for the way you are always willing to share the precious gift of time... for always believing in the best in people... for always seeing the bright side of things... for the many kind words you have spoken... for the thoughtful things you have done... The world needs more people like you!

Consider Yourself Hugged

...by Me!

Imagine me wrapping my arms around you with my heart. I am so happy that you are a part of my life! Consider yourself hugged!

You Are a Friend

I Will Always Cherish

When I think of our friendship, I realize that it is one of the things I cherish the most in my life. It is hard to put into words a "thank you" with enough meaning for all the times you have come through for me... for all the times you have listened instead of telling me what to do... for all the times you have hugged away my troubles... for the laughs over nothing... for the many tears dried. Thank you for it all, my special, cherished friend!

About Marci

Marci began her career by hand painting floral designs on clothing. No one was more surprised than she was when one day, in a single burst of inspiration and a completely new and different art style, her delightful characters sprang from her pen! "Their wild and crazy hair is a sign of strength," she thought, "and their crooked little smiles are endearing." She quickly identified the charming characters as Mother, Daughter, Sister, Father, Son, Friend, and so on until all the people and places in life were filled. Then, with her own loved ones in mind, she wrote a true and special sentiment to each one. This would be the beginning of a wonderful success story, which today still finds Marci writing each and every one of her verses in this same personal way.

Marci is a self-taught artist who has always enjoyed writing and art. She is thrilled to see how her delightful characters and universal messages of love have touched the hearts and lives of people everywhere. Her distinctive designs can also be found on Blue Mountain Arts greeting cards, calendars, bookmarks, and other gift items.

To learn more about Marci, look for Children of the Inner Light on Facebook or visit her website: www.MARCIonline.com.